For those who suffer and for those who seek to find a cure.

C.S.

JORDAN TANG

THINK ... CREATE ... DISCOVER

CHERYL SCHUERMANN

I AM OKLAHOMA
CHILDREN'S SERIES

SERIES EDITOR: GINI MOORE CAMPBELL

OKLAHOMA HALL *of* FAME
OKLAHOMA HERITAGE ASSOCIATION PUBLISHING

OKLAHOMA HALL *of* FAME

2015 OFFICERS AND DIRECTORS

Unless otherwise noted, photos courtesy of the Oklahoma Hall of Fame.

©2015 Oklahoma Heritage Association Publishing, a publication of the Oklahoma Hall of Fame

Printed in Canada
ISBN: 978-1-938923-20-3
LIBRARY OF CONGRESS CONTROL NUMBER: 2015948202

Book and Cover Design: Skip McKinstry

JORDAN TANG
THINK ... CREATE ... DISCOVER

Chapter I   A Young Man's Dream

The young scientist looked up from his notebook. Could it be? Is this the secret he had been looking for? He had worked day after day, month after month, year after year. He asked the questions. He ran the experiments. And recorded his observations. He had been careful and patient. He looked back at his data. After seven years, Jordan Tang had finally solved the puzzle. "I've done it!" he cried. And, for a short time, he was the only one in the world who knew about it.

When he solved this puzzle, the young scientist was a long way from his home in Taiwan. Jordan Tang arrived in Oklahoma in 1955 with a dream to study science. He wanted to make important discoveries.

Jordan had $200 in his pocket for college. His father had gathered some of the money. Several other families from his village added their money. They wanted to help Jordan follow his dream to study in the United States. They all believed Jordan would do great things. And, they were right.

Oklahoma Medical Research Foundation (OMRF) was started in 1946. The scientists there try to understand human illnesses. Then, they work to find a cure. They focus on important research areas such as Alzheimer's disease, cancer, and heart disease.

Dr. Jordan Tang is a world class **research scientist**. He has been at Oklahoma Medical Research Foundation for over fifty years. Dr. Tang has studied several important diseases. And, he has made many important discoveries. His work in the **laboratory** is the first step to finding cures for disease.

"This is probably the biggest thrill a scientist can have, to see his work on its way to treat and help people. Researchers live for moments like these, because they are so few and far between."

Dr. Jordan Tang

Chapter 2   An Inventor is Born

Jordan Tang was born in 1931 in Fuchow, China. When he was six years old, Japan invaded China. Jordan went to live with relatives. His parents wanted to protect their children from danger. The children later returned to their parents.

The family moved from town to town to stay away from the war. Jordan attended many elementary schools. Some were very small schools with only one room.

Jordan Tang was born in Fuchow, China. His family later moved to the island of Taiwan.

The children did not have many books to read. One day, their father brought home a book about Thomas Edison. Jordan and his brother read about the famous inventor again and again. They read about the light bulb and the phonograph. The boys found a blank notebook. They wrote a title in big letters on the front—INVENTION BOOK.

"My brain was not made to remember details. My brain was made to think up new ideas, create, and make connections."
Dr. Jordan Tang

A young Jordan Tang with his family in China. Jordan is standing second from the left.

Jordan and his brother thought of many inventions. They drew pictures of their ideas in the notebook. One of their ideas was to make a long, wide belt. Rollers on each end would turn. This caused the belt to move along. It would be a "people mover." Many years later when

Jordan traveled to the United States, guess what he saw? People movers! Jordan rode on escalators and moving sidewalks at airports.

When the war ended, Jordan's father moved his family to Taiwan. Jordan attended high school there. A good education was important to his family. But, Jordan's teachers noted that he was not very good at memorizing facts. His mind was thinking beyond the facts. He was always inventing and creating.

Jordan studied about soils and crops in college. Then, he worked for the Fertilizer Ministry. Someone discovered he was good at drawing and painting. So, he painted posters for farmers. The posters showed how to make crops bigger and better.

Jordan was a gifted artist. But, he had a dream. Soon, that dream would take him half-way around the world.

A full 20% of the world's population live in China. In other words, one in every five people on the planet live there. China is almost as big as the entire United States. Taiwan is only $\frac{1}{5}$ the size of Oklahoma.

Chapter 3   Oklahoma Bound

Jordan Tang left Taiwan in 1955 to attend school in Oklahoma. He traveled by ship to North America.

Jordan Tang wanted to study in the United States. But, where? East coast? West coast? He looked for a good science school. He decided on Oklahoma State University (OSU). With $200 in his pocket, Jordan was ready for a big adventure. He packed a suitcase. Then, he said goodbye to his family and homeland.

Jordan flew on a plane to Japan. Then, he boarded a ship named *Yu-San*. Twenty-one other students were going to America, too. They became good friends. They celebrated the Chinese New Year on the ship by eating Chinese dumplings.

Thirteen days later, the ship arrived in Canada. Right away, Jordan and his new friends met the next challenge. The language! Jordan did not know many English words. And, most people he met did not know *any* of his language. Jordan knew "cheese" and "sandwich." So, that is what he ordered at restaurants.

The bus ride from Canada to Oklahoma City took almost forty-eight hours. Then, Jordan rode another bus to Stillwater. He thought the buildings were very beautiful. And, that the Americans were very rich. He met many other students from China. Jordan loved college life. But, soon he was busy with his studies.

On the other side of the globe, his village in Taiwan cheered him on. Hopes were high. But none in the village could even *imagine* what Jordan Tang would achieve.

The Chinese New Year is an important Chinese holiday. It is also known as the Spring Festival. It is the longest festival in China. The holiday may include special family meals, decorating the house, and lighting firecrackers.

Photo courtesy Skip McKinstry.

"College life was great fun at the beginning as there were so many new things to learn. But soon I had no time to notice these things as I was immersed totally in my study and work. This eventually led to a long scientific career." Dr. Jordan Tang

Jordan Tang studied **biochemistry** in college. This is the study of things that are inside of us. A **biochemist** tries to understand how life works. Jordan wanted to understand health and disease. He learned what happens when we eat and how our bodies use food. He learned about **cells** and what happens inside those cells.

Jordan enjoyed his first winter on the Oklahoma State University campus. He played in snow for the first time.

Chapter 4   Thrill of Discovery

While at OSU, Jordan met Kuen, the girl of his dreams. He first saw her in a research lab. Kuen, pronounced Quinn, and Jordan had attended the same high school in Taiwan. But, they did not know each other there.

Jordan Tang received his master's degree in 1957. He wanted to continue his studies at the University of Oklahoma Health Sciences Center in Oklahoma City. The next year, he became a student. Before moving to Oklahoma City, he made plans to share his life with Kuen.

Jordan Tang met his future wife, Kuen, at Oklahoma State University. They were married in Oklahoma City in 1958.

Enzymes are very, very small. They cannot be seen with even the most powerful microscope. Sometimes, as many as 1,000 enzymes can be inside one cell. Enzymes are workers! They do a lot of the work that is going on in a cell. When a cell needs to get something done, it almost always uses an enzyme to speed things up. If enzymes do not work properly, a person can become ill.

Jordan Tang joined the Oklahoma Medical Research Foundation in 1957. Soon, he would make his first major discovery in the lab.

Jordan began working in the lab at Oklahoma Medical Research Foundation. If they were happy with his work, he would get a raise after three months. Well, he got his raise. *And*, lots of attention.

During Jordan's first month in the research lab, he made a discovery. He found a new **enzyme** (en-zime) in the human stomach. An enzyme is a very small part of a **cell**. It cannot be seen with a microscope. No one knew this one existed!

Jordan wrote about the new enzyme. This helped other scientists make a test for stomach cancer. The test has saved many lives. This discovery excited Jordan. He wanted to know more about how our bodies work.

Dr. Tang is a distinguished medical research scientist. He is not a medical doctor. He discovers ways medical doctors can help their patients get well.

> *"My goal as a scientist is to do more research, find out more, and hopefully make another breakthrough."*
> Dr. Jordan Tang

Dr. Tang's graduation day in 1961. He earned a Ph.D. in Biochemistry from the University of Oklahoma.

Jordan and Kuen were married in June, 1958. Kuen worked in the same lab as Jordan. While working, Jordan continued his training. He received a Ph.D. in Biochemistry in 1961.

In 1965, they moved to England for further study. But, Oklahoma wanted Dr. Tang back. The following year, he became a full-time scientist at OMRF. By then, he and his wife had two young boys, Albert and Joseph.

Chapter 5   Think Like a Scientist

How does a scientist think? According to Dr. Tang, it all starts with **curiosity**. He asks a question. He wants to know how something works or how it can be better.

When Dr. Tang discovered the new enzyme in the stomach, he did not stop there. He asked, "How does this enzyme in the stomach help digest our food?" After understanding that, he asked more questions. "Where else does this enzyme work in a similar way?" He tested his **hypothesis** with experiments. Then, he studied the results. He did this same process over and over again.

Where do research scientists think and explore? And create? And discover? A laboratory is the perfect place.

You may not know it, but you think like a scientist every day. Are you curious about something? A question comes up and you try to find an answer. Do you think about what you already know? Do you make inferences, or educated guesses? Do you make predictions, come up with a plan, and see if your plan works? When you ask questions and try to solve problems, you are thinking like a scientist.

Most laboratories look similar. The rooms are clean and well-scrubbed. Bright lights hang overhead. Masks, goggles, gloves, and white coats are by the door. Modern instruments sit on the counters along with stacks of round dishes, called **petri dishes**. A large assortment of glass test tubes, plastic tubing, and all sorts of bottles are within reach.

With every experiment, a scientist learns something new. But, what if the experiment does not work? The scientist can learn as much from what *does not* work as from what does work! This is the process of building knowledge—one piece of information at a time.

Dr. Tang measures liquid into a petri dish. He makes sure his measurements are accurate.

Test tubes are very useful in the lab. Scientists hold, mix, or heat small quantities of liquids or chemicals in test tubes.

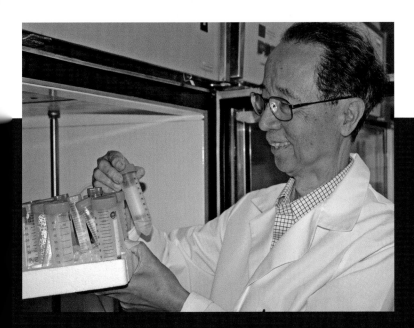

Dr. Tang wants every young scientist to know ...

Scientific research takes patience. Often, basic experiments are done day in and day out without knowing how the results will be used. Providing just one more piece of the puzzle may result in a major breakthrough.

Dr. Tang's laboratory has many different types of equipment. They aid in his research.

Dr. Tang with his model of the enzyme, pepsin. The model took several years to create.

Models can be very helpful in understanding a difficult topic. For example, a favorite model to make in school is the solar system. By using styrofoam balls, string, toothpicks, and different colored paints, students can make a model of the planets that will help them understand how the solar system works.

In the same way, Dr. Tang made models of the structure of enzymes. These are 3-D shapes magnified millions of times. They help him and other scientists see things that are difficult to understand.

Chapter 6   Making Connections

A scientist never stops asking meaningful questions. Dr. Tang found a new enzyme in the stomach. Then, he wanted to learn more. He chased the enzyme to a cell. He chased it to the bloodstream.

"What are the connections?" he wondered. He made **three dimensional** models of the enzymes. Models help scientists understand complex things in a simpler way.

Dr. Tang learned more and more about how the body *should* work. Most enzymes help the body work better. But, some can be an enemy to the body.

He studied another enzyme. He asked questions. He made predictions and did the experiments. And, he made a huge discovery! The "work" this enzyme was doing caused some people to become very sick.

"Research is not easy. Usually you find what won't work. I have been lucky to have a few really meaningful findings."
Dr. Jordan Tang

Dr. Tang adjusts the equipment in his laboratory.
The machines help him by mixing, measuring,
and analyzing the enzymes he is studying.

This new information gave other scientists a "map" to follow. Once they knew what was going wrong, they could make medicines to help the person stay well. In other words, they knew the enemy. They found its weakness. Then, created a plan to defeat it. Because of Dr. Tang's work, millions of people have been helped. His research has led to treatment for several diseases.

In science, one discovery leads to another. In 1999, Dr. Tang found a new enzyme and named it *memapsin 2* (me-map-sin). The enzyme was not working right in the body. He believed it was the cause of Alzheimer's (awltz-high-merz) disease. This disease damages the brain and robs people of their memory.

"Sculpture Park at Night" was featured in an art show in Norman, Oklahoma in 2006.

Chapter 7   Another Side to Dr. Tang

As a young man, Dr. Tang did not choose art as a career. But art and music have been a big part of his life. "Art is tremendously satisfying to me," he said. "When I create a piece of art, I enjoy both the product and the work. I love the creativity."

Dr. Tang does not sell his oil paintings. They are sometimes used to raise money to help other people. One of his art shows was called "Memories." It featured paintings by Dr. Tang and another artist. Money from the show went to Alzheimer's research.

When viewing one of Dr. Tang's paintings, people often ask him, "What's going on?" His reply is always the same. "What do *you* think is going on?"

"Most artists paint with feeling. I paint with ideas and thinking, a lot like I do research."

Dr. Jordan Tang

Dr. Tang's oil painting "Painting on Location" shows a fun outing with a group of artists.

"Painting On Location"
Oil
Jordan Tang

For many years, scientists have thought that science and music are connected. In 2010, seven scientists from OMRF volunteered for an amazing experiment. They had only ten days to learn about writing music and compose an original piece for a string quartet. Dr. Jordan Tang was one of those scientists. His composition, "Scientist," was performed before a live audience at the Oklahoma City Museum of Art.

Dr. Tang believes this is the same thinking process a scientist goes through when forming a hypothesis. *What do you think is going on?*

Dr. Tang is on the board of directors of the Oklahoma City Museum of Art. He has also worked with the Oklahoma Arts Institute. Dr. Tang plays the piano, mainly classical music. He even wrote a musical composition for a string quartet. It is called ... what else? "Scientist!"

Dr. Tang's artwork is considered to be abstract. Abstract Art is a non-lifelike picture of real world objects, people, and scenes.

Dr. Tang has lectured and taught around the world. His goal is to share his knowledge with others so they can make new discoveries, too.

"In science, knowledge is power. To know what something does starts our curiosity and love for finding new things. You have to learn how to generate ideas, how to push the frontier of our knowledge. And how to push the boundaries."

Dr. Jordan Tang

Chapter 8   The Research Continues

The world took notice when Dr. Tang discovered memapsin 2. Other scientists knew right away what this meant. Millions of people with Alzheimer's disease could be helped. Or, even cured. Dr. Tang found the cause of the disease. Since then, he has worked on a cure.

In 2001, Dr. Tang received a big research prize. The Alzheimer's Association gave him the Pioneer Award worth one million dollars. This money helped him continue his work. Since that time, Dr. Tang has received millions more for his research.

When talking about OMRF, Dr. Tang smiled. "I think their spirit came from the American West idea that anything was possible," he said. "Oklahomans have that spirit."

The Tang family: Kuen, Albert, Dr. Tang, and Joseph. Albert and Joseph live and work in Texas.

Dr. Tang is often asked to speak about his discoveries. He has spoken at fifty colleges on five continents. He has written more than 200 articles for science journals. Dr. Tang hopes to inspire young scientists to think, create, and discover.

He and his wife live in Edmond, Oklahoma. When asked about his state, he quickly responded. "Oklahoma means everything to me. It is my home."

And Oklahomans are proud to call Dr. Jordan Tang their own.

Dr. Tang holds a 3-D model of the enzyme, memapsin 2. This is the enzyme found to be the cause of Alzheimer's disease.

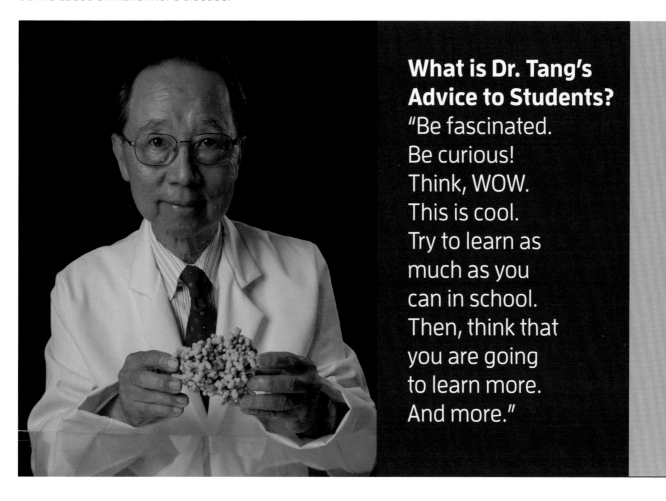

What is Dr. Tang's Advice to Students?

"Be fascinated. Be curious! Think, WOW. This is cool. Try to learn as much as you can in school. Then, think that you are going to learn more. And more."

Glossary

biochemist	a person who studies how living things are made and how they work
biochemistry	the chemistry of living things
cell	the basic unit of all organisms
chemistry	science that teaches us how things are made and what they are made of
curiosity	the desire to learn or know about anything
enzyme	workers in living cells that can cause changes, as in digesting food
hypothesis	a statement about what might happen based on evidence plus prior knowledge
laboratory	a place for experiments, investigating, and observation
petri dish	a shallow glass dish used for growing very small organisms
research	careful investigation into something in order to discover facts
scientist	a person who gains knowledge of the world by observing and experimenting
three-dimensional	life-like or real, also known as 3-D

Timeline

1931	born in Fuchow, China
1946	moved to Taiwan with his family
1955	traveled to Oklahoma to attend Oklahoma State University
1957	graduated with a master's degree in Biochemistry
1957	began work at Oklahoma Medical Research Foundation
1958	married Kuen
1958	attended University of Oklahoma
1961	completed Ph.D. in Biochemistry at the University of Oklahoma
1961	Albert was born
1963	Joseph was born
1965	moved to England for research
1966	returned to Oklahoma to work as a research scientist at OMRF
1982	named Chair of Medical Research by the Puterbaugh Foundation
1999	discovered memapsin 2, the key to Alzheimer's disease
2001	received the $1 million Pioneer Award for research
2001	inducted into the OSU Hall of Fame
2008	inducted into the Oklahoma Hall of Fame

Dr. Jordan Tang, left, received Oklahoma's highest honor when he was inducted into the Oklahoma Hall of Fame. He was presented for induction by Dr. Stephen M. Prescott.

The Scientific Method

The scientific method is a way to ask and answer scientific questions by doing experiments and making observations. This is how we think like a scientist!

Here are the six steps:

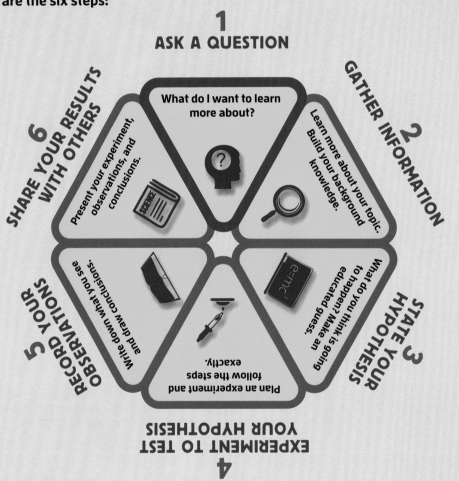

1 ASK A QUESTION

What do I want to learn more about?

2 GATHER INFORMATION

Learn more about your topic. Build your background knowledge.

3 STATE YOUR HYPOTHESIS

What do you think is going to happen? Make an educated guess.

4 EXPERIMENT TO TEST YOUR HYPOTHESIS

Plan an experiment and follow the steps exactly.

5 RECORD YOUR OBSERVATIONS

Write down what you see and draw conclusions.

6 SHARE YOUR RESULTS WITH OTHERS

Present your experiment, observations, and conclusions.

36

Want To Learn More?

Places to Visit

Science Museum Oklahoma
2100 N. E. 52nd Street
Oklahoma City, Oklahoma 73111
sciencemuseumok.org

Tulsa Children's Museum
Discovery Lab
560 Maybelle Avenue
Tulsa, Oklahoma 74127
tulsachildrensmuseum.org

Leonardo's Children's Museum
& Adventure Quest
200 E. Maple
Enid, Oklahoma 73701
leonardos.org

Jasmine Moran Children's Museum
1714 Highway 9 West
Seminole, Oklahoma 74868
jasminemoran.com

Museum of the Great Plains
601 NW Ferris Ave
Lawton Oklahoma 73507
discovermgp.org

Oklahoma Hall of Fame at the
Gaylord-Pickens Museum
1400 Classen Drive
Oklahoma City, Oklahoma 73106
OklahomaHOF.com

Oklahoma Historical Society and
Oklahoma History Center
800 Nazih Zuhdi Dr.
Oklahoma City, Oklahoma 73105
okhistory.org

Teachers' Guides for the I AM OKLAHOMA CHILDREN'S SERIES available at OklahomaHOF.com under the Education tab.

Online Information

http://kids.usa.gov/science/
>   Learn more about inventors and scientists.
>   Get some great ideas for your next science fair project.

www.chem4kids.com
>   An excellent resource for basic chemistry help and information.

www.biology4kids.com
>   Information about living things, how they work, and how they change.

www.oklahomahof.com
>   Information on Oklahoma's rich history and heritage.
>   Explore members of the Oklahoma Hall of Fame.

Index

Author Biography

Cheryl Schuermann is a reading specialist and published author. She taught school for many years and now works as an education consultant. Cheryl wants every student she meets to love reading and learning. When she is not in schools or writing, she can be found having fun with her thirteen grandchildren.

Cheryl has always admired the work done by medical research scientists. Every family in the world is affected by illness and disease in some way. By reading about Dr. Jordan Tang, Cheryl hopes students will be inspired to think ... create ... and discover.